COMPUTER PROGRAMS AND CODING

Please visit our website, www.garethstevens.com.
For a free color catalog of all our high-quality books,
call toll free 1-800-542-2595 or fax 1-877-542-2596.

Cataloging-in-Publication Data

Names: Dickmann, Nancy.
Title: Computer programs and coding / Nancy Dickmann.
Description: New York : Gareth Stevens Publishing, 2020. | Series: Computing for kids | Includes glossary and index.
Identifiers: ISBN 9781538252550 (pbk.) | ISBN 9781538252567 (library bound)
Subjects: LCSH: Computer programming--Juvenile literature.
Classification: LCC QA76.52 D49 2020 | DDC 005.1--dc23

Published in 2020 by
Gareth Stevens Publishing
111 East 14th Street, Suite 349
New York, NY 10003

For Brown Bear Books Ltd:
Text and Editor: Nancy Dickmann
Children's Publisher: Anne O'Daly
Design Manager: Keith Davis
Designer and illustrator: Supriya Sahai
Picture Manager: Sophie Mortimer
Concept development: Square and Circus

Printed in the United States of America

CPSIA compliance information: Batch #CS20GS: For further information contact Gareth Stevens, New York, New York at 1-800-542-2595.

Picture credits: Front Cover: Shutterstock; Interior: iStock: Daisy-Daisy 5; Shutterstock: Arica Studio 6, Alba Alioth 8, BillDayOne 19, PT Casimiro 21, Everett Historical 9, Frame Stock Footage 7, 12, Gorodenkoff 16, 26, Alesia Kan 10, LightField Studios 17, Monkey Business Images 24, 27, NicoElNino 13, Zoran Orcik 14, Phil's Mommy 25, Pira 23, Andrey Popov 4, Pressmaster 15, Sylwia Ramach 22, Rawpixel.com 18, WaveBreakMedia 11; U.S. Government: U.S. Navy/James S. Davis 20.

Words in the glossary appear in bold type the first time they are used in the text.

CONTENTS

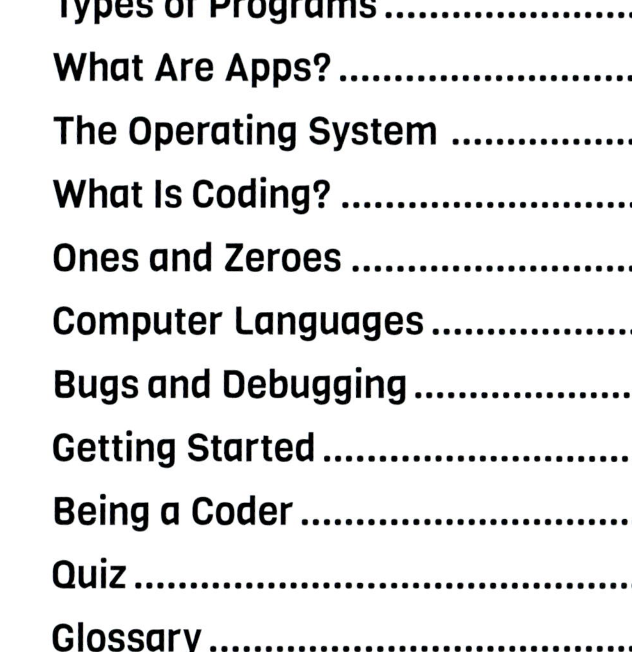

01

INSTRUCTIONS NEEDED!

Clicking with a mouse is one way to give a computer instructions.

How do you get a computer to do what you want it to?

Computers can do a lot of things. They can add numbers, play videos, and send messages. But they can't think for themselves. If you want a computer to do a job, you must give it clear instructions.

Make it clear

A computer works in a logical way. It processes **commands** one by one. This means the commands have to follow a pattern. If a step is left out, or put in the wrong order, the computer can't guess what it is supposed to do.

Some homes have a digital assistant, which can hear and respond to your spoken instructions.

When you ask a digital assistant to play music or look up a fact, you are giving it instructions.

{ }

01

ALGORITHMS AND PROGRAMS

To perform a task, a computer will use something called an algorithm.

That name might sound pretty complicated! But an algorithm is simply a list of rules to follow in order to do a job. A recipe for a cake is a sort of algorithm. So is a set of instructions for building a toy or model.

The steps in a dance routine are in order, like an algorithm.

Computer algorithms help scientists track and forecast weather.

Computer programs

An algorithm can tell a computer how to use **data**. The algorithm must be turned into a computer **program**. This means putting it into a **computer language** (a language the computer understands).

Search engines use complicated algorithms to choose the best matches for your web search.

THE FIRST PROGRAMS

It took a while for people to figure out how to make computer programs.

In the 1800s, an inventor was able to program a **loom** for weaving cloth. He fed the machine cards with holes punched in them. The machine "read" the cards to create fabric with complicated patterns.

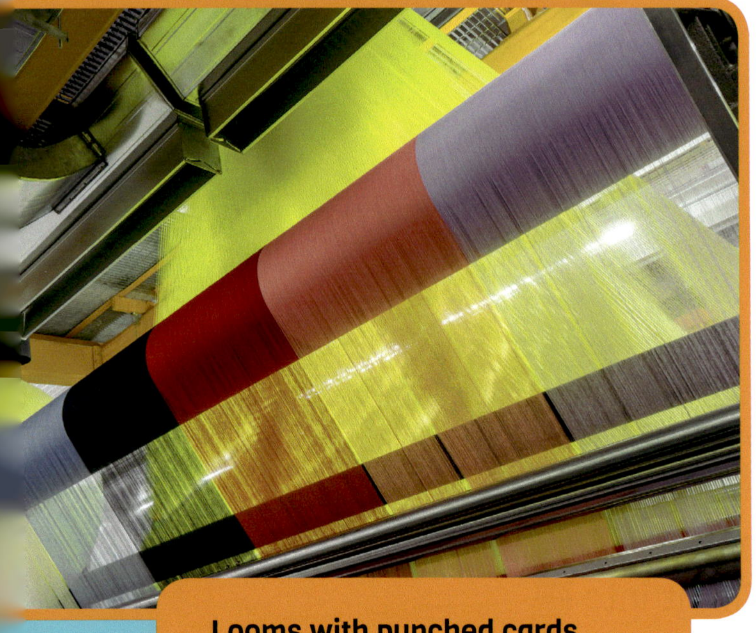

Looms with punched cards made it quick and easy to create beautiful fabric.

Punch cards

In the 1950s, early computers used **punch cards**. At the time, punch cards were the only way of storing computer files and programs. A computer program could take up a whole stack of punch cards.

The punch cards in a computer program had to be kept in the right order.

Special machines were used to make computer punch cards.

TYPES OF PROGRAMS

For every job that a computer needs to do, there is a program to tell it how to do it.

Computer programs control the way that a robot moves.

Some programs are part of the computer's basic system. They control how the different parts of the computer work together. Other programs can be installed (put on) later. They each do a specific job, like editing music files or organizing numbers.

Statements

All types of computer programs use statements. A statement is a command, such as “print” or “**input**.” A computer program puts several statements together to form an instruction. The computer performs each command.

A computer starts with the first statement in a program and then does the rest in order.

A computer program is a bit like a book. If you read it in the wrong order, it won't make any sense.

WHAT ARE APPS?

Animation applications help filmmakers create exciting scenes.

When you think of a computer program, you are probably thinking of an application.

Spreadsheets, games, **browsers**, calendars, and editing programs are all applications. People use them every day for work or for entertainment. Each application on a computer does a different job.

A mapping app uses your phone's location system to show you where you are.

Mini computers

Smartphones and tablets are small computers. They run applications, too. People usually call these "apps." When you want to run one, you tap its **icon** on the homescreen. You can use apps to shop, look up train times, play games, or edit photos.

Apps can make use of a phone's built-in features, such as the camera.

01

THE OPERATING SYSTEM

The most important program on any computer is the operating system.

The **operating system** manages the different applications. It starts them running. It controls how they interact with other parts of the computer, such as the keyboard or mouse.

The head chef in a restaurant manages the cooks in the same way that an operating system manages applications.

User interface

You interact with your computer through something called the "user interface." This is the arrangement of icons, windows, and menus that you see on the screen. The user interface lets you store and access files. It is part of the operating system.

The operating system controls accounts and passwords, to keep your data safe.

A user interface makes it easy to keep files and applications organized.

WHAT IS CODING?

We use computer programs every day. Coders are the people who write them!

Computer programs are made up of **code**. Code is words and numbers that form a set of instructions. Coding is the process of writing code that a computer can understand. It is how we make computer programs.

When you code, you often type instructions on a computer.

Coding rules

To work properly, code has to follow certain rules. It has to be in a language that the computer recognizes. It has to be in the right order. It can't ask the computer to do things that are impossible.

A woman named Ada Lovelace created the first computer program in 1843.

A recipe follows an ordered pattern, just like computer code does.

{ }

01

ONES AND ZEROES

A computer must understand code in order to follow any instructions it's given.

A computer can't understand English. It can't understand French or Chinese either. A computer only understands electrical signals. These signals have two possible positions. They can be on, or they can be off.

It doesn't matter what language you speak—a computer only understands numbers.

All computer code gets turned into a long string of ones and zeroes.

Binary

A computer takes in information as a string of ones and zeroes. This is called **binary**. A one represents “on,” and a zero is “off.” When a computer reads a line of code, it automatically converts the letters and numbers into binary.

To a computer, “01001000” means “H” and “01001001” means “I.”

COMPUTER LANGUAGES

Admiral Grace Hopper was one of the first coders. She invented a computer language called COBOL.

Coders don't write in ones and zeroes. They use a computer language.

There are hundreds of different computer languages. Like a spoken language, each one has its own words, terms, and symbols. It also has rules for how those elements are put together. This makes instructions that a computer can understand.

Like many computer languages, Python is based on English.

Choosing a Language

A coder chooses the best language for the project. Some computer languages are good for games. Others are better for building websites or making programs that **analyze** data. Complicated programs might use a mix of different languages.

Some of the best-known computer languages are Swift, HTML, C++, Java, and Python.

01

BUGS AND DEBUGGING

If a program won't run, coders have to find and fix any errors.

Computer games go through lots of debugging before they are put on sale.

Everyone makes mistakes, and sometimes coders make a mistake in the code they write. These mistakes are called "**bugs**." Finding and fixing them is called "**debugging**." The errors could be spelling mistakes or lines of code in the wrong order.

Get it right!

If you write a story and misspell a word or leave out a period, your teacher will still understand what you meant. But a computer can't do this. Even the tiniest mistake, such as forgetting to close a bracket, can mean that a program won't run.

Once, scientists found a real bug (a moth) inside a computer. The bug kept it from working.

Code editing programs can help coders find and fix bugs.

GETTING STARTED

Sharing ideas with a friend is a great way to plan a simple game, such as a maze.

Getting started with computer coding is easier than you think!

With just a bit of help and practice, anyone can code simple games and animations. The first step is to plan what you want your program to do. Then think about the steps involved and what order they will need to go in.

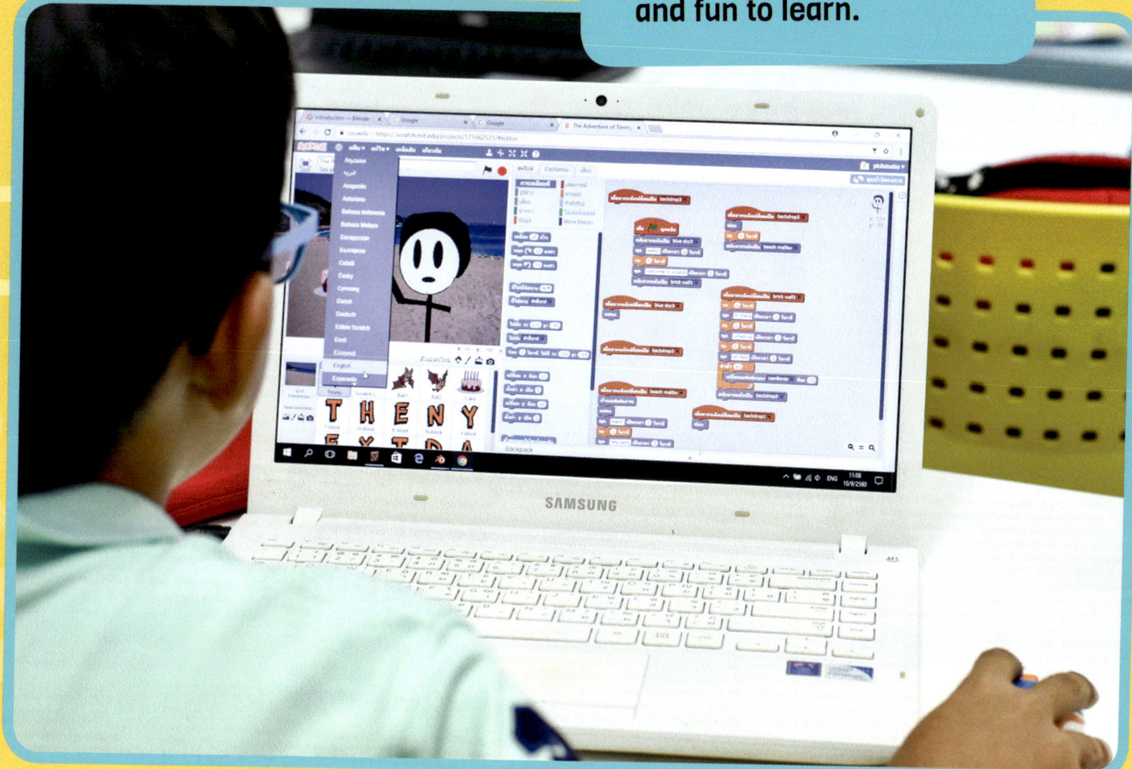

Coding in Scratch is easy and fun to learn.

Scratch

Many children start coding by using a simple language such as Scratch. In Scratch, you can drag and drop blocks that contain code. By putting these blocks together, you can create a list of instructions for characters or objects, called "sprites."

Kodu is another easy programming tool that is similar to Scratch.

{ }

01

BEING A CODER

Many coders find jobs developing new computer games.

There are many jobs available for people who are good at coding.

Coders can do a huge range of jobs. They can develop new computer programs and apps. They can design games, build websites, or set up computer networks. Most coders specialize in one area. They become experts in the computer languages that those jobs need.

Computer security

Some coders specialize in testing computer programs. They look for weaknesses in the code and fix them. A weakness might let hackers in. Hackers are people who illegally break into computer systems.

The number of girls and women doing computer coding is going up.

Lessons and workshops are a fun way to practice coding and learn new skills.

QUIZ

Try this quiz and test your knowledge of coding and computer programs! **The answers are on page 32.**

1. What is an algorithm?

a. an electrical part found inside a computer

b. a list of rules to follow in order to do a job

c. a spicy Middle Eastern soup

2. What were early punch cards used for?

a. automatically weaving patterns into cloth

b. voting in elections

c. choosing meals at a restaurant

3. Which of the following are applications?

a. keyboards, screens, and wires

b. apples, carrots, and potatoes

c. games, spreadsheets, and browsers

4. What does an operating system do?

a. it manages the different applications on a computer

b. it performs surgery automatically, without a doctor

c. it turns on the lights when you enter a room

5. Which of these is a computer able to understand?

a. German and Spanish

b. ones and zeroes

c. music and sculpture

6. What is debugging?

a. finding and fixing errors in a computer program

b. cleaning dust and grit out of a computer

c. swatting any mosquitoes that come near

7. Why is Scratch an easy language to learn?

a. it only has ten different words

b. it has blocks of code that you can drag and drop in place

c. it can be used on a smartphone

8. Which of these jobs can a coder do?

a. manage the chefs in a restaurant kitchen

b. send secret messages

c. develop new games and applications

GLOSSARY

algorithm a process or list of rules to follow in order to do a job

analyze to examine something in detail

application a computer program designed to do a particular job

binary a system of ones and zeroes that can be used to represent letters and numbers

browsers computer programs used for accessing and interacting with websites

bugs errors in a computer program or system

code a system of letters and symbols used as instructions for a computer

commands orders or instructions given to a computer

computer language a language that is used in programming computers

data information that is stored or used in a computer, in the form of a series of ones and zeroes

debugging finding and fixing errors in computer programs

icon a symbol that represents a computer application on a screen

input something that is put into a system

loom a machine used for weaving threads into cloth

operating system the program that controls a computer's basic functions and keeps its parts working together

program a set of coded instructions for a computer to follow

punch cards cards with holes punched into them that were once used to program computers

search engines programs that find particular websites on the internet

spreadsheet a type of computer program that arranges data in rows and columns

FIND OUT MORE

Books

Gifford, Clive. *Awesome Algorithms and Creative Coding (Get Connected to Digital Literacy).* New York: Crabtree Publishing Company, 2015.

Pratt, Mary K. *What Is Computer Coding? (Lightning Bolt Books – Our Digital World).* Minneapolis, MN: Lerner Publications, 2015.

Scott, Mark. *A Beginner's Guide to Coding.* New York: Bloomsbury Children's, 2017.

Wainewright, Max. *How to Code: A Step-By-Step Guide to Computer Coding.* New York: Sterling Children's Books, 2016.

Websites

Go here to find answers to questions about computers:
www.bbc.com/bitesize/subjects/zyhbwmn

Learn more details about computer programming:
www.dkfindout.com/uk/computer-coding/

This website has free online coding courses and activities:
studio.code.org/courses

This website will get you started coding in Scratch:
scratch.mit.edu

This video explains more about debugging:
www.bbc.com/bitesize/articles/ztkx6sg

INDEX

Quiz answers
1. b; 2. a; 3. c; 4. a; 5. b; 6. a; 7. b; 8. c